Meditations
for
Tough and Testing Times

Meditations
for
Tough and Testing Times

Rev. Dr. Bernard R. Wilson

iUniverse, Inc.
New York Lincoln Shanghai

Meditations for Tough and Testing Times

iUniverse books may be ordered through booksellers or by contacting:

iUniverse
2021 Pine Lake Road, Suite 100
Lincoln, NE 68512
www.iuniverse.com
1-800-Authors (1-800-288-4677)

With the blessing and support of:
The Norfield Congregational Church
64 Norfield Road
Weston, Connecticut, 06883

Unless otherwise indicated, the passages of scripture appearing at the beginning of each meditation are from:
THE MESSAGE: *The Bible in Contemporary Language*
Copyright © 2002 by Eugene H. Peterson
NavPress Publishing Group

ISBN-13: 978-0-595-39234-6 (pbk)
ISBN-13: 978-0-595-83626-0 (cloth)
ISBN-13: 978-0-595-83625-3 (ebk)
ISBN-10: 0-595-39234-2 (pbk)
ISBN-10: 0-595-83626-7 (cloth)
ISBN-10: 0-595-83625-9 (ebk)

Printed in the United States of America

To my parents
Deacon David R. Wilson
and
Mother Dovetta Wilson,
Who taught their
nine children to do all the good we can,
for all the people we can,
in every way we can,
while we can.
In every way,
and every day,
I will endeavor to continue their legacy.

I also want to thank my brother, Charles,
and my sisters, the Rev. Carolyn C. Blair and the Rev. Dr. Ruby Wilson,
for their work on this book.

Special thanks to Ellen Dickinson and Crystal Curcio-Bonner for making my
words better.

And always,
Nereida,
Michael,
Daniel,
and Mia Jean…
In every thing and every way, it's all for you.

Contents

Foreword by
Rev. Dr. Ruby Wilson

It is an exciting privilege and honor to introduce this classic book of meditations by Rev. Dr. Bernard R. Wilson. I have known Rev. Wilson all of my life, for not only is he my blood brother, but he is my spiritual brother, mentor, and friend. As I read this book, I found that I had to treat it as if I were eating an elephant, taking and savoring one bite at a time. The deep, rich nuggets found on each page have kept me reflecting on the Word of God.

This is a book with twenty-five gems. The meditations found within these pages provide fresh insight into God's Word. Take time to prayerfully read one gem from this book as you begin your day, or during a break—while waiting for something or someone, or when opening your Bible study class. You will find yourself refreshed, renewed, revived, delivered, set free, and transformed!

These meditations from Rev. Wilson, a true visionary for our time, will show you that when a believer walks with Christ, a flash of the world eternal swallows up the world of the here and now. It is in these moments that the believer can celebrate and rejoice in what is to come.

This book will enrich your life regardless of who you are, where you have come from, where you have been, or what you have done. The nuggets in these pages will provide you with spiritual enlightenment that tells you that we serve a God who is able to create new things even out of our old conditions.

Be challenged, and experience God anew as God speaks through God's messenger, the Rev. Dr. Bernard R. Wilson, in *Meditations for Tough and Testing Times.*

Rev. Dr. Ruby Wilson, Pastor
Safe Haven United Church of Christ, New York

Foreword by
Rev. Carolyn C. Blair

This book of meditations by my brother, the Rev. Dr. Bernard R. Wilson, is a real testament to our mother, Dovetta. Bernard is the son she called "Rev" from the time he was born, convinced that God had called him to the Gospel ministry. As I read my brother's meditations, I could not help thinking of our mom who raised us in tough and testing times.

The power of a mother's enduring faith and love beams from the souls of her children as they live their own lives, raise their own families, and teach others about the power of faith in God. Our mom instilled in us a deep and abiding trust in the Lord, in preparation for the challenges and circumstances she knew we would we face in life. All nine of us had ample opportunity to watch, and *learn from*, her faith in action.

Through times of trouble, when the Wilson family struggled through the discrimination of the 1950s, the poverty, riots, and the war in Vietnam during the 1960s, Mom held on to a deep faith that God would see us through. It was Mom's faith that brought our dad, David Wilson, Sr., a nonbeliever, into the fold. Dad gave his life to Christ. Healed from a tumor, he dedicated the last decade of his life not only to his family but also to the church, and he faithfully attended Sunday services, taught Sunday school, and led Bible Study. It was Mom's faith and her loving discipline and encouragement that helped her children learn to make appropriate choices and to reject opportunities to turn to drugs, so rampant in the Harlem community in which we lived. Mom's faith encouraged us to put God first, pursue education, and become giving citizens of our nation. What we learned from Mom and Dad, and what my brother shares in these meditations, is: lean on the Lord, believe in the power of prayer, and trust that prayer changes things. What I know you will come to realize (as you reflect on these wonderful meditations and the classic prayers by my brother Chaplain Charles Wilson) is that when you face tough and testing times, you ought to hold onto your principles and maintain your faith. These words of faith and trust in the God we know in Jesus Christ will not only inspire you, but will also motivate you to believe that all things are possible if you believe and have faith. May God bless the reading of these words in your life.

Rev. Carolyn C. Blair, C.A.S., M.S.Ed.

Introduction

◆

In Tough and Testing Times

Build houses and settle down;
plant gardens and eat what they produce.
Marry and have sons and daughters;
find wives for your sons and give your daughters in marriage,
so that they too may have sons and daughters.
Increase in number there; do not decrease.
Also, seek the peace and prosperity of the city to which I have carried you into
exile.
Pray to the LORD for it, because if it prospers, you too will prosper.
(New International Version, Jer. 29:5–7)

Star Trek: Voyager is one of my favorite television series. *Voyager* is about a crew that, through a catastrophic event of futuristic science, finds itself alone in an unknown galaxy far, far, away from home.

They have no idea what the dangers that face them may be, and the only way back to Earth will take at least seventy years. What to do? They can pray for a miracle, find a planet and settle down, or they can begin their long journey home. The ship's captain, Kathryn Janeway, points her ship and crew toward home to begin the seventy-year journey. Captain Janeway tells the crew that when you face "tough and testing times, you hold onto your principles and maintain your faith."

We are living in tough and testing times—times when we feel as though we cannot control what is happening around us; and times when we are uncertain about how to cope with today and are afraid of what tomorrow might bring. We are faced with the question: do we believe God is faithful to us in tough and testing times?

The collapse of the World Trade Center and the attack on the Pentagon—symbols of stability and might—left the people of the United States, and the world, uncertain, unsure and afraid. The events of September 11, 2001, placed the international community in times that tested our lives. Testing times make us anxious and afraid about the places where we sleep, the restaurants in which we eat, and the airplanes we board. In tough and testing times we turn to God.

In testing times, we stand by our faith because our hope is built on more than buildings, weapons, and declarations. Our hope is built on nothing less than the Eternal God of the Universe. Our hope is in the God who has the power to drive out chaos, confusion and those who seek to terrorize our lives. Through faith in God we find that anchor of certainty our lives desperately need.

For many years I have been asked to share my thoughts and insights on faith, the Bible, and God's action in our lives and in our world. During my installation as Senior Minister of the Norfield Congregational Church, my brother Charles, who penned the wonderful prayers for each of the meditations in this book, challenged the congregation to encourage me to publish these meditations. The people of Norfield took up the challenge, and now this book represents my response to their encouragement.

Norfield is a wonderful place. Here is a congregation in affluent Weston, Connecticut, with a 98 percent Caucasian membership that willingly and unanimously crossed the color divide and called an African American minister born in Harlem to pastor them. I have learned much from my pastorate here at Norfield. And I know now, more than ever, that God's people want to know about the God who loves them and how to live the life that God is calling them to in tough times.

The messages contained herein reflect the theology of my faith. I believe that God loves and cares for each and every one of us, and that in tough and testing times, we have the blessed assurance that God demonstrated Divine Love by sending Jesus Christ to sacrifice His life for us—all of us. We can celebrate that we serve a God who is active in our lives and our world. I am convinced that the Bible offers us a way to live the life that God created for us.

When preparing messages and meditations, I try to visualize those individuals who I know are in need of an encouraging and life-giving word from God: I see the man who is struggling with addictions of various kinds; the teenagers confused about their lives and what God expects of them; the woman worried about her marriage and the role God wants for her in the world; the couple left uncertain, after losing a source of income, about whether or not they will be able to make ends meet; and the individual aging faster than he or she ever imagined, and now facing the reality of death.

All of these men and women facing their own personal challenges are searching for divine assurance. They are not alone. No matter the situation that may confront us as a community of faith, God is there: through devastating hurricanes, catastrophic tsunamis, and brutal acts of terrorism. Despite the suffering, the pain, and the failures that plague us, the God we know through Jesus Christ is a shelter from the storm. God acts on our behalf and is faithful through all of our trials.

What can "trust in God" offer? Trusting in God empowers us in these tough and testing times, enabling us to keep the faith and ensure the dignity of all God's children. So, while the nations of the world prepare to release the dogs of war, we remain confident because we know that the kingdom of this world is already the Kingdom of our Lord God. Our hope is in the God who reigns forever! May these meditations remind you of God's faithful and abiding love.

1

Divine Possibilities for You

Then Moses summoned Joshua. He said to him with all Israel watching, "Be strong. Take courage. You will enter the land with this people, this land that God promised their ancestors that he'd give them. You will make them the proud possessors of it. God is striding ahead of you. He's right there with you. He won't let you down; he won't leave you. Don't be intimidated. Don't worry."
(Deut. 31:7–8)

Moses must have been an inspiring mentor for Joshua. There had to be something about the leadership Joshua saw in Moses that so enthralled him and thus allowed him to follow in the footsteps of his teacher.

Perhaps it was the scene at the Red Sea, where God parted the waters for the Hebrew people, allowing them to escape the tyranny and wrath of their Egyptian oppressors. Or it may have been when Joshua saw Moses return after receiving the Ten Commandments. Whatever it was, it greatly moved Joshua and challenged him to pick up the mantle of Moses and lead God's people into the Promised Land.

Every one of us needs a mentor, someone who *motivates* us to use our God-given talents for service; who then *monitors* our development, in order for us to *multiply* the community of believers so that we can then become mentors for others.

I think of the mentors in my own life:

- my father, David R. Wilson, Sr. When I was a little boy, I watched him get up and go to work every morning so he could care for his nine children, because it was his responsibility to do so;

- my mother, Dovetta Wilson, understood the importance of family and faith and instilled that in her children. She insisted that her children become responsible citizens capable of taking care of themselves;

- Mr. George, the drugstore owner, gave me a job and taught me the importance of getting to work on time—and the significance of calling when I couldn't make it. He put the onus on me to come to him and ask for a raise if I wanted to get one;

- Ms. Batya Lewton, the school librarian at P.S.197 of Harlem, tutored me on weekends, taught me the joys of reading, and infused within me a desire to learn; and

- Bishop Milton Perry, who spoke to me of the Divine Possibilities for my life and encouraged me to preach in the spirit of God.

We all need teachers and mentors who can help us see what God can do through us if we open our hearts, minds, and lives to the leading and the spirit of God. We all have a responsibility to become teachers and mentors ourselves; to reach out and make the world a better place to live.

God has instilled within each of us that which must be agitated in order to come forth from within us. The Apostle Paul urged Timothy to "...stir up the gift that is within you." That gift is the Divine Possibilities which "...equip the saints for the work of ministry, for the building up of the body of Christ, until all of us come to the unity of the faith and of the knowledge of the Son of God" (New Revised Standard Version, Eph. 4:12–13).

We must take these words of Martin Luther King, Jr., to heart:

> If I can help somebody as I pass along...
> If I can cheer someone with a word or song...
> If I can show someone they're traveling wrong,
> Then *my* living will not be in vain.

O Lord, our Lord,
How majestic is Your name!
The great provider, the sustainer, the mentor
Who leads us into Divine Possibilities.

Prepare us for service,
Guide our feet as we run this race.
Bring others into the Kingdom,
Built on love,
Sustained by truth,
Blessed with hope.

Send us out to lead others into the Kingdom.
Equip us, O God, to see the Divine Possibilities
In others and ourselves.

We ask of You these things this day,
Amen.

2

Keeping Faith

Are you the One we've been expecting, or are we still waiting?
(Matt. 11:2–3)

During a trip to South Africa as part of Norfield's International Outreach Ministry and Ambassadors for the Town of Weston, the Team worked with South Africans, many of whom were homeless, hungry, handicapped, helpless, HIV/AIDS afflicted, and, in some cases, hopeless.

At one clinic we met and listened to a woman named Sulatene[1], a woman from Masi, who was diagnosed with HIV in 1999. Sulatene, the mother of a nine year old boy, spoke to us about what it is like living with HIV/AIDS and knowing that death is near. She spoke to us about how it is to realize that you will be leaving your child alone in the world. Sulatene's husband kicked her out of their home once he found out she was infected with the dreaded virus, despite the likely possibility that she contracted the disease from him. Shunned by her husband, ostracized by family and friends, condemned by her community, Sulatene sought solace in her faith as she struggled with the tough and testing times before her. She wondered if the God she knew in Jesus Christ was the God she should serve, or if some other Divine being could deliver her from her challenges.

Sulatene reminds me of John the Baptist. John falls into the category of people with what I call the "H-Factor"—those who are Homeless, Hungry, Hated, Handicapped, Helpless, and/or Hopeless. Today we can add those who are struggling with HIV/AIDS, like Sulatene. These are the people in our society we often label unworthy of our care. Most of the time, we wish that they would go away or be silent so that we don't have to witness their sufferings. Several years ago in New York City there was a major thrust to move the homeless out of the subways and ferry stations, so that commuters would not have to see them on their way to work.

---

1.   Names have been changed.

John the Baptist was counted among the homeless and hated. He lived in the wilderness; was hated for the things he said; hated for the way he said them; and hated for his appearance.

When we encounter him in Matthew 11:3, John the Baptist is sitting alone in a prison, struggling with his ministry, questioning his calling, and wondering if his life and preaching have made any difference at all. In an attempt to cope with this depressing situation, John sends his disciples to Jesus and poses this piercing question: "Are you the One we've been expecting, or are we still waiting?"

Now, coming from any other individual in the New Testament, this inquiry would not be a surprising one; however, from John the Baptist it is an amazing question because this is the same man who demonstrated such absolute conviction that Jesus was the One in the first chapter of John.

> The very next day John saw Jesus coming toward him and yelled out, "Here he is, God's Passover Lamb! He forgives the sins of the world! This is the man I've been talking about, 'the One who comes after me but is really ahead of me.' I knew nothing about who he was—only this: that my task has been to get Israel ready to recognize him as the God-Revealer. That is why I came here baptizing with water, giving you a good bath and scrubbing sins from your life so you can get a fresh start with God."
>
> John clinched his witness with this: "I watched the Spirit, like a dove flying down out of the sky, making himself at home in him. I repeat, I know nothing about him except this: The One who authorized me to baptize with water told me, 'The One on whom you see the Spirit come down and stay, this One will baptize with the Holy Spirit.' That's exactly what I saw happen, and I'm telling you, there's no question about it: This is the Son of God."

To pose the question, "Are you the One we've been expecting, or are we still waiting?" seems out of John's character. But John has been through a great deal and now, as he is sitting in prison awaiting his execution, John isn't certain that Jesus is the One. When we go through tough and testing times, it is all too easy to lose faith. When we are struggling, we all wonder if God is walking with us. We wonder if our Lord is going to see us through the challenges that we face. So we can understand why John, in his moment of crisis, sends this trenchant question to Jesus: "Are you the One we've been expecting, or are we still waiting?"

The answer John receives in Matthew 11:4–6 is a key to our understanding of who we are and the calling that has been placed upon us as followers of Christ. Jesus responds to John's question by telling John's disciples to:

> Go back and tell John what's going on
> The blind see,
> The lame walk,
> Lepers are cleansed,
> The deaf hear,
> The dead are raised,
> The wretched of the earth learn that God is on their side.

Today, Jesus would want the community of the faithful to be able to say:

> The homeless are finding places to live!
> The hated are finding love!
> The helpless are finding hope!
> The handicapped are being motivated!
> The hungry are able to feed themselves!
> And today's lepers, those who have HIV/AIDS, are being delivered from their disease!

Jesus would challenge us to keep the faith, follow His example, and embrace everyone in the spirit of God's love. May it be so in our world today!

Great God of the Universe,
My soul magnifies Your Name!
Great are You, and greatly to be praised!
There is none like You, O God,
Quick to show mercy, slow to anger, quick in justice.
Forgive us for being quick to judge,
Fast to avenge, and slow in justice.
Forgive us for neglecting the abused:
The poor, the hurting, the molested,
The homeless, the sick...
Give us the spirit of faith, forgiveness, and love.
Lord, help us to see the beauty and joy in everyone.
Give us that radical love of Jesus,
The love that makes hatred vanish;
The love that is demanding to all;
The love that removes bitterness, envy, and strife;
The love that makes us uncomfortable
Until we find rest in You,
To be the servants You've called us to be,
And to treat everybody right.

In Jesus' love,
Amen.

3

Where Are You?

*When they heard the sound of God strolling in the garden in the evening
breeze, the Man and his Wife hid in the trees of the garden, hid from God.
God called to the Man: "Where are you?"*
(Gen. 3:8–9)

My father, David R. Wilson, Sr., always paused whenever he came across
questions in the Bible. Dad discovered that where a question is raised, the story is
probably taking a sudden turn, or a crucial action is taking place. It is a moment
in the story when the reader can find the essence of the text.

The particular passage in the text from Genesis 3 bears out Dad's discovery. In
fact, I am convinced that the entire Bible is a response to this question asked in
the first Book:

Where are you?

Something I discovered about this question posed by God to the first human
is that Adam immediately understood what God was asking. Adam didn't try to
filibuster by answering, "God, all you have to do is turn left at the third tree on
the right and then walk two bushes down to the last tree." No, Adam answered
the question truthfully:

I heard you in the garden and I was afraid because I was naked. And I hid.

This is the essence that runs through every book of the Bible, the notion that
God has lost something and wants it back! The Lord God is seeking *A-dam*[1],
God's *human* creation, to bring humans back into a right relationship with the
Eternal God of the Universe. In Luke 19:10, Jesus said this was the entire reason
for His coming:

---

1.   Adam (A-dam) is a Hebrew word for "man" or "human."

For the Son of Man came to find and restore the lost.

The question God poses to Adam in the garden is the same question you must ask of yourself: "Where are you?"

Where are you in your relationship with God?
Where are you in your faith-walk?
Where are you physically? Is all well with your body?
Where are you professionally? Are you growing and adapting to your ever-changing environment?

As we move about our lives from that Garden called Eden, God continues to pose this question to you and me: "Where are you?"

The answer is crucial, because it speaks to our spiritual place as a people of faith. Have we sinned as Adam did? Do we need to return to a right relationship with God? If so, now is the time of salvation.

Lord,
We come to You "dressed down,"
Believing that You are impressed
With our accomplishments,
Enamored of our eloquence, delighted by our degrees,
Proud of our titles, awed by our physical appearances.

Lord,
We come to You "dressed up,"
Believing that You are impressed with
The gold and glitter of our achievements,
The rubies and diamonds of our skills,
The pearls and gems of our mastery...

So, O Lord,
Strip us today of our devotion to our possessions.
Let us come before You as newborn babies,
Naked, wanting Your care and nurture.
Find us in Your perfect will,
Dress us in Your love,
Help us to be a people of faith,
Filled with Your presence.

In Christ's name,
Amen.

4

Let There Be Light

In the beginning God created the heavens and the earth.
Now the earth was formless and empty,
darkness was over the surface of the deep,
and the Spirit of God was hovering over the waters.
And God said, "Let there be light," and there was light.
(NIV, Gen. 1:1–3)

Just what did God mean when these four words were spoken?

Let there be light!

The easy answer is that God turned on the sun and set it burning in the sky, but that is too simplistic an answer, because sunlight came later in the creation process, appearing on the fourth day. So what did it mean when God said "Let there be light"? Perhaps God meant to create a new way of seeing and perceiving, or a new way of believing.

The creation process is much like the birthing experience: bloody, messy, and painful. When my sons, Michael and Daniel, were born, I took those opportunities to share in the experience with my wife (as much as a man can share in that process). I heard much screaming and witnessed much blood. It was no small effort, I realized, to bring forth life into the world. As in the moment when God said, "Let there be light," things changed for me. My perception of life was altered. Who I was before my sons were born was different from who I was afterward. It is like the old Gospel song that says:

Something got a hold of me
When I went to the church that night,
and my heart wasn't right,
Something got a hold of me.

> 'Cause afterwards when I looked at
> my hands, my hands looked new
> When I looked at my feet, they did too
> When I started to walk, I had a new walk,
> And when I started to talk, I had a new talk.

Not that I had new hands or new feet, but the way I looked at myself was different after the Spirit got ahold of me.

Now, it is important to bear in mind that "Let there be light" does not mean "let there be no darkness," but "let there be a time of light, let there be a time for darkness, and remember that light comes from darkness *and* darkness comes from light." When light is declared, there is a period of spiritual adjustment—just as your eyes adjust when you move from light into darkness and from darkness into light. When light is declared in your life, you must allow for that period of change.

Let there be light calls upon us to see ourselves in new ways.

Let there be light calls us to accept new visions, new ideas, and creative and redemptive ministries.

Let there be light calls us to see the institution and the people we serve, regardless of their race, gender, color, or sexual orientation. The Heavenly Gift of Light calls us to see others as people in need of God's love and care, who may need new light for their lives.

Let there be light asks us to see our nations and their governments as well as the need for clarity and direction in the policies and laws they shape.

In these tough and testing times, we need to understand that when light comes, old things pass away and, behold, all things are new.

O God,
Creator of night and day,
Darkness and light,
Open our eyes that we may see
The brightness of Your love...
Rebuke the darkness of despair.
Rebuke the demons in our minds.
Rebuke the spirit of fear and criticism.

Lord,
Impart in us the spirit of light.
Help us to see the light of God,
And the glory of Christ!
Open our eyes
That we may see the beauty in ourselves,
In others, and in You.
Let there be a willingness to see Christ,
The Light of the world,
Who has caused us to walk in the light,
To be truth-tellers, love-spreaders,
Justice shapers, and burden sharers.
Remove our shame,
And let us walk boldly to the Throne
Where Grace abounds.

In Jesus' name,
Amen.

5

A New Beginning

Suddenly, God's angel stood among them and God's glory blazed around them. They were terrified. The angel said, "Don't be afraid. I'm here to announce a great and joyful event that is meant for everybody, worldwide: A Savior has just been born in David's town, a Savior who is Messiah and Master."
(Luke 2:8–12)

It seems like not too long ago when the breakup of Prince Charles and Princess Diana headlined newspapers worldwide. It was such a significant event for us because of the hope that we invest in those who occupy positions of prominence and authority. We hoped that Charles and Diana's storybook wedding would turn out to be a storybook marriage and life. We hoped they would inspire us with their love and that our fantasies for their love would be fulfilled. Instead, our hopes were dashed as the realities of their lives moved from a royal wedding to a royal divorce and ultimately, to a royal death. What we learned from Charles and Diana is that their regal heritage did not shield them from the common, confusing complexities of modern life that each of us struggle with daily.

We frequently invest the same sorts of hopes in all of our leaders and persons of fame. Whenever a new president, governor, or mayor is elected, a new commanding officer is assigned, or a new pastor is called to a church, that same sense of renewal, change, and hope fills the air.

When John F. Kennedy was inaugurated as President of the United States, he spoke of his inauguration as an "…end, as well as a beginning—signifying renewal, as well as change." Former U.S. President Bill Clinton spoke of his own inauguration as "…American renewal and reunion—a new beginning for all." Yes, we know and we understand that neither a president nor any other leader can do it all, but there is always hope that *just maybe* things will get better.

The Advent season of the Christian faith is another time of renewal and hope. Every year we speak of the coming of a Savior who brings joy to the world. This

14

Savior brings the kind of joy that fills the hearts and minds and souls of all humanity and reminds us of our responsibilities to each other. During Advent we recall the Phillip Brooks hymn:

> O little town of Bethlehem, how still we see thee lie.
> Above thy deep and dreamless sleep
> the silent stars go by.
> Yet in thy dark streets shineth the everlasting light
> The hopes and fears of all the years
> are met in thee tonight.

"The hopes and fears of all the years" come to mind as fighting wages on in Iraq and Afghanistan. They come to mind as we watch people who are hungry and dying in Africa; as terrorism sweeps across the planet; and as AIDS takes its toll on people around the globe. Yet, in Advent we find ourselves in a season of hope. And unlike the hope we place in humans—be they American presidents, European monarchs, African tribal chiefs, Japanese emperors, or any individual in a position of leadership worldwide—the confidence we place in that baby born in a manger in that little town of Bethlehem gives us strength for today and hope for tomorrow.

O Lord of new beginnings,
Keep us from being stale and cold!

O Lord of new beginnings,
Keep us from losing our creativity!

O Lord of new beginnings,
Remove the shame and fear
That prevent us from freely loving You!

O Lord of new beginnings,
Restore relationships once healthy and strong!

O Lord of new beginnings,
Renew our commitment for service
To the Kingdom of God.

O Lord of new beginnings,
Bring us back to the place where
We received You as Lord and Savior,
So from the old we can be made new,
Alive in Christ,
To worship and serve You.

Amen.

6

Be Still!

Be still, and know that I am God;
I will be exalted among the nations,
I will be exalted in the earth.
(NIV, Ps. 46:10)

A group of children confined indoors on a rainy day create a game to see how many tacks each can pry loose from the furniture in the house. Each of them works feverishly, prying and gathering as many tacks as possible. And when the sun finally comes out, they leave with their pockets full of tacks and the furniture all in shambles.

There are times in our lives when we too allow ourselves to engage in self-indulgent behavior, distracting ourselves with time-consuming, yet unproductive, activities. We become like these children, defined in part by our greedy attempts to get as much as we can, in any way we can. Unfortunately, too often, all we have to show for how we've lived are tacks. What a waste of God's precious gift of life!

Reflecting on ourselves, we frequently feel as though we have been leading wasted lives—lives without purpose, direction, or meaning. Lives without any sense of where water might be found—water: the one ingredient that turns a wasteland into a green land teeming with life.

People can be busy while living in a wasteland—busy, but not getting much out of life. Moving, but not seeming to get anywhere. Working, but failing to accomplish much. Yes, people can be baffled and confused wanderers who are moving aimlessly through life, while doing nothing with the precious gift of life God has given.

In such busy, harried, stress-filled lives, what is it that can give significance and meaning to our hurried existence? What is it that can serve as our water, our sustenance, and make our daily experiences teem with life?

Perhaps the words of the psalmist provide the best answer:

Be still, and know that I am God!

It isn't easy to be still while seeking to make a living, is it? Downsizing, budget cuts, and lifestyle changes keep each of us ever on the go. And so stillness must be created in order for us to experience the place of peace, serenity, and calmness to which the psalmist calls us with the words: "Be still!"

We can find this stillness in a lily pond or a running brook; the crashing of the waves against the shore; a dogwood tree; a home in which everything is in its proper place, so that the effect of simple order makes everything restful. I often tell my wife, Nereida, that whenever the bed is rumpled and the sheets have slipped from the sides of the bed, it disturbs my night terribly and makes me feel as if I have been sleeping in mass confusion. For me, as for so many others, superficial disorder makes us feel out of order on the inside. So we need to create order around us to keep from feeling off-kilter.

Most effective, however, is the creation of order within us. The psalmist advises us to somehow create places of quiet in our hearts; places that, despite the busy-ness and noisiness, give us rest from all the turmoil, tension, and disorder of our lives.

Billy Graham was once asked what he would do differently if he could live his life over again. Would he study more? Preach more? Teach more? Travel more? Conduct more revivals? Dr. Graham's answer was plain and simple: he said that he would pray more. He would find more time to be alone with God.

Be still! From the hectic and frantic pace of life.
Be still! From the many projects, meetings and deadlines imposed upon you.
Be still! From the stress and strain of living.
Be still! From confusion and disorder in your life.

Be still and know!

The only way for us to become what God intends for us to be, and sent Jesus so that we might be, is to, "Be still and know that God is God."

And if we practice this kind of stillness, it will transform our lives. It will be in these moments of stillness that the words of Psalm 46:1–9 (NIV) will ring clear for us:

God is our refuge and strength,
an ever-present help in trouble.
Therefore we will not fear, though the earth give way

> and the mountains fall into the heart of the sea,
> though its waters roar and foam
> and the mountains quake with their surging.
> There is a river whose streams make glad the city of God,
> the holy place where the Most High dwells.
> God is within her, she will not fall;
> God will help her at break of day.
> Nations are in uproar, kingdoms fall;
> he lifts his voice, the earth melts.
> The LORD Almighty is with us;
> the God of Jacob is our fortress.
> Come and see the works of the LORD,
> the desolations he has brought on the earth.
> He makes wars cease to the ends of the earth;
> he breaks the bow and shatters the spear,
> he burns the shields with fire.

The psalmist tells us that God is exalted among the nations and the earth, and instructs us clearly to:

> Be still and know that God is God.

Lord,
Help us to get rid of the clutter that is within us—
The clutter that keeps us from being all we can be.
Help us to see that we are more
Than nerves, tissues, flesh, and blood...
But souls, needing to cry out to You
For purpose and direction.

Help us to be still,
To listen to the still, small Voice
That speaks deep within our souls,
To cast our cares upon You,
Because You care for us.

In the stillness of the hour,
May we hear the music playing,
The birds chirping, the wind whispering,
And may we hear You speaking
The Voice of truth and reconciliation,
Telling Your children to come home
To peace, safety, and refuge...

Amen.

7

What Sign Shall We Follow?

Tell us, when are these things going to happen?
What will be the sign of your coming, that the time's up?
(Matt. 24:3)

The northwestern Native Americans erected totem poles with carved emblems (*totems*) which represented their clan or family. The carvings often depicted creatures that were believed to give strength, that showed their family line, or that identified who they were. These totems were revered and held sacred by succeeding generations.

All of us erect totems and wear symbols that represent what we stand for, what we believe in, or what we are willing to die for: the cross, for our God; the national flag, for our country; the red ribbon, for our identification with those who have died or are suffering from AIDS.

Very often, we idolize things that we believe crystallize who we are: our athletic skills or musical talents, our profession or our sources of income, our personal interests or hobbies.

All of these totems have one thing in common: they are images of our Selves, so we honor them and defend them with our very lives because, for us, they *are* our lives. But in the Hebrew text we are instructed—no, we are *commanded*—by God to make no graven images.

That is to say, nothing in our lives should take precedence over the God we serve. Nothing in our experiences should equal the Eternal God of the Universe. Nothing that we own or achieve or fear should become our God. Not the church we attend. Not the Bibles we read. Not even the crosses we wear around our necks should be greater than God. These objects can only point to God, because God can never be trapped in a thing or a place.

Jesus did not give us totems to worship but, rather, signposts to follow. The Star of Bethlehem was a signpost that pointed to a babe who lay in a manger. John the Baptist was a signpost pointing to the Lamb who would take away the sins of the world. In Matthew 24, Jesus gave us signs which would point to His return: wars and rumors of wars, earthquakes in different places, the sun refusing to shine, and the moon dripping in blood.

But Christ reminds us not to become fixated on the signs but to use them to guide us through the maze of life. Jesus directs us to pull down the totem poles that we've erected to show how great and glorious we are. Christ asks us to follow the signposts God has provided, which lead us to be humble about who we are, and to seek God's redemption. The signs point us to God's Kingdom and the new life that God gives.

God gives us signs, but we often ignore them. Why? Because they don't help us make money or make us great in the eyes of others. But God's signs encourage us and give us strength for today and hope for tomorrow. God's signs help us to remember who is in control of our world and our lives. God's signs remind us that the sufferings of today cannot compare to the Glory which has been prepared for those of us who are faithful followers of God's Word.

Our prayer should always be:

God, open our eyes that we might see Your great works and glorify You.

God who leads us,
God who guides us,
Keep us from clannish and selfish worship:
Of ourselves,
Of our little trinkets,
Of our society,
Of our income.

Lead us by Your signposts
As we journey home.

Amen.

8

Who Am I?

When Elijah saw how things were,
he ran for dear life...
(1 Kgs. 19:3)

People we respect and admire are people who know who they are and do not pretend to be anything other than that. We all know people who set out to be in the limelight, to win friends and influence people; the kind of individuals who want to be more than what they are. We tend to shy away from these people who seem to be insecure about their identity. But people who know themselves are at liberty to share themselves with others honestly, sincerely, and with great integrity. Each of us should ask: *Who am I?*

I offer four responses to this question:

We are who we think we are.

Who we see in the mirror every morning determines many of our actions. If you see yourself as a victim, people will exploit you. If you see yourself as a leader, people will follow you. If you see yourself as a child of God with gifts, talents, insights, and God-given abilities, then you will bring joy and inspiration to yourself and to others. And if we are who we think we are, then we can say to ourselves: I can grow! I can change! I can do better! We can, with God's help, be better.

We are as others see us.

Jesus was the great Identifier of potential. When others saw Simon as a flaky, insecure disciple standing on shifting sand, Jesus saw Peter the Rock. When others saw a downtrodden harlot from Samaria, Jesus saw an Evangelist who could bring others into the Kingdom. When others saw a wild, crazy individual who spent his days and nights in the tombs, Jesus saw a man who simply needed Divine direction and purpose for his life.

I thank God for my parents and my mentors. They saw something in me, a little kid from Harlem, and provided the guidance I needed. The drugstore owner who gave me a job because he thought he could trust me. The Superintendent of High Schools in New York City, Dr. James Boffman, who refused to permit me to drop out of school because he thought there was something in me that even I could not see.

Once we gain a glimpse of how others see us, we are very often motivated to keep from letting them down. We strive to realize our potential because we are given a new perspective, a new way of seeing ourselves, through the eyes of others. Once that greatness in us is named, it is up to us to act on the best that we find within.

We are what we do.

Life has meaning when it takes on purpose and has goals to fulfill. If we are what we do, we have no excuse for avoiding responsibility for our lives and failing to making a difference in the lives of others. There is no excuse, even if the possibility remains that those to whom we reach out may never return the good we offer them. This point was made clear for me when I was ready to attend college. Funds were too low for me to go. My pastor, Bishop W.J. Robinson of the Garden of Prayer Cathedral Church of God in Christ, did more than his share to ensure that while I was away at school, I had money on which to survive. He ensured that I had the funds to go back and forth between school and home during vacation. At one time, Bishop Robinson started to tell me that he was looking forward to the day when I would return the blessings I was receiving from him, but stopped short before he completed the sentence. Instead, he said, "you may never return to help us, but God will bless our church through others." He told me to follow God's leading in ministry and that God would bless both the church and me—and boy, was he right! His efforts speak volumes about challenging others to do and be something in life.

We are what we believe.

Life is a journey for all of us. The goal is different for everyone. We must learn to appreciate the journey as we move through it. That means appreciating sweet, hard life with all of its triumphs and tragedies, successes and sorrows, hopes and horrors, and conflicts and contradictions. We must participate in the whirlwind of despair. We must learn to stand fast during the earthquakes of confusion and be prepared for fiery trials. We must keep searching in order to hear the still, small voice of God speak to us about our lives and purpose here on earth. We can only achieve this by a constant nurturing of our faith in God.

Elijah's experience in 1 Kings 19:8–12 has a message for us:

> He got up, ate and drank his fill, and set out.
> Nourished by that meal, he walked forty days and nights,
>   all the way to the mountain of God...
> When he got there, he crawled into a cave and went to sleep.
> Then the word of God came to him: "So Elijah, what are you doing here?"
> "I've been working my heart out for the God-of-the-Angel-Armies," said Elijah.
> "The people of Israel have abandoned your covenant, destroyed the places of worship, and murdered your prophets. I'm the only one left, and now they're trying to kill me."
> Then he was told,
> "Go, stand on the mountain at attention before God. God will pass by."
> A hurricane wind ripped through the mountains and shattered the rocks before God,
>   but God wasn't to be found in the wind;
> after the wind an earthquake,
>   but God wasn't in the earthquake;
> and after the earthquake fire,
>   but God wasn't in the fire;
> and after the fire a gentle and quiet whisper.

Through knowing ourselves, we become a people whom God can and will use. It is the "gentle and quiet whisper" that prods us forward in our journey of life and comforts us when times are tough.

"I am thine, O Lord,
I have heard Your voice,
And it told my love to You,
But I long to rise in the arms of faith,
And be closer drawn to You!
Draw me nearer,
Nearer, blessed Lord,
To the cross where You have died,
To Your precious bleeding side!"[1]

Lord, I forget I belong to You.
So I make decisions without seeking You.
I search for answers without consulting You.
I depend on others, who fail me and let me down.
I've done things my way,
And I feel lost, not knowing who I am.

Let me give up my searching to know who I am,
And surrender to the One
Who is greater than my thoughts,
Deeper than my feelings,
And higher than my intellect,
And I give You praise
For knowing me better than I know myself...

Amen.

---

1. Fanny J. Crosby, "Draw Me Nearer," 1875.

9

Jesus, What Do You Want With Us?

Jesus? Nazarene! I know what you're up to!
You're the Holy One of God,
and you've come to destroy us!
(Mark 1:23–24)

Are there really demons in the world today? In ancient times, demons were a common foe. They frequently attacked and wreaked havoc on the community. One example is Legion (the demon's name, not the unfortunate host), who possessed a man so that he was put in the cemetery by the community and often ripped up the tombstones, tore off his clothing, broke his chains, and streaked through town.

We don't believe that we have demons like Legion in today's world. Today, we are an "enlightened" people. We believe if we can simply get so-called "demon-possessed" people the appropriate help by trying to understand their predicament—knowing how cruel their parents were or how tough their socio-economic deprivation has been, for example—we can solve their problems. There's no need, we think, to talk about demonic possession in today's world.

Yet, can we really believe that our drug problem is *not* a result of demonic forces? Is the individual who rapes innocent children and terrorizes innocent people not afflicted with some sort of demon? Can the constant barrage of hatred that fills our airwaves and permeates our society not be fueled by some kind of demonic possession? Can we who are much too concerned with self-image, sex, money, and all the petty things we consider important, not be possessed by some type of demon? Are all of these signs of decadence a result of some force that simply is not of God? If there is such a thing as demonic possession, is there a word from the Lord that helps us to deal with this affliction?

That Word is from the Gospel of Mark. It begins with Jesus announcing the Good News. Something takes place that will forever change the lives of God's people. It's something so exciting and so new that people will be willing to leave all and follow Jesus as He goes about teaching the Good News of God's action in the world.

Now, we know there was something strange about this Jesus of Nazareth. When He traveled, crowds followed; when He spoke, people listened; when He acted, changes took place; when He laid His hand upon the sick, they were healed; when He prayed, food was multiplied; when He walked, the waters supported His weight; and when He taught, people were amazed at His teachings, for He taught as one with authority.

On this particular occasion, Jesus is in the synagogue teaching, when a man possessed with a demonic spirit rises and cries out:

> What business do you have here with us, Jesus?

It is a question that people have asked of Jesus since His coming more than two thousand years ago. "What business do you have, Jesus, what do you want with us?" Herod thought Jesus wanted his earthly kingdom. The disciples thought He wanted to establish a new kingdom on earth. The Pharisees and scribes were worried about losing their authority and influence and thought Jesus wanted to diminish the power they held over people.

> What business do you have here with us, Jesus?

Unfortunately, we've often answered this question in a narrow and simplistic way: "Jesus wants me to read my Bible more, pray more, do more." But the Bible provides a clear picture of what God wants. The prophet Micah tells us what God requires of us: do justice, love kindness, and walk humbly with our God (NSRV, Mic. 6:8). Jesus tells us: "Love the Lord your God with all your passion and prayer and intelligence; Love others as well as you love yourself" (Matt. 22:37–40).

Confronted by the demon in the synagogue, Jesus sternly responds, "Quiet! Get out of him!" The Bible says that when Jesus uttered this command, the man shook violently and the evil spirit came out of him with a shriek.

The Good News is that Jesus is still casting out the demons in our lives. The Good News is that Jesus was sent so that those demons within us can be released if we are willing to accept His teachings and His truths. That acceptance sets us free to do what God calls us to do. The Good News is that because Jesus was crucified for our hang-ups, we don't have to get hung up anymore.

The Good News is that God's love, as shown in Jesus Christ, frees us from all the demons within us.

Great God of glory,
Commit us to service.
As You send rain to water the land,
Send Your Holy Spirit to prepare us for harvest,
Yes, to prepare us for service.

Forgive us for serving other Gods,
The gods of this world, the gods of pride,
The gods of wealth and status,
The gods of self.

Turn us around to serve others,
To bring peace to the troubled,
Hope to the hurting,
Food to the needy,
Shelter to the homeless...

In Jesus' name,
Amen.

10

All May Change

Early in the morning on the first day of the week, while it was still dark,
Mary Magdalene came to the tomb and saw that the stone was moved away
from the entrance. She ran at once to Simon Peter and the other disciple, the
one Jesus loved, breathlessly panting, "They took the Master from the tomb.
We don't know where they've put him."
(John 20:1–2)

We live in a rapidly changing world. In fact, the world we were born into no longer exists. Many things we did as children simply are no longer done. Technology has advanced, knowledge has increased, and information moves at such a speed that the world is even smaller than it once was.

A poem I learned as a child reads:

> The world was larger once when time was slow
> Hundreds of years and continents ago
> Columbus sailed into an endless west
> The world was larger then by every test.
> What China did, no one in Europe knew
> 'Til weeks and months and even years were through.

The remarkable growth of technology and the increasingly rapid rate of change tend to unsettle us, upsetting our equilibrium. Unfettered change makes the future uncertain and frightening because we are unsure of what it holds. We are uncertain we will be able to cope with the future when it arrives. If we cannot be certain of what the future brings, it is unclear what we should hold fast to, or value. Deep inside we are afraid that in the process of change, something of worth will be lost.

In the text from John 20, Mary Magdalene is confronted with a change of cosmic proportion. Her world has crumbled. What she has learned to depend upon and value most, her relationship with Jesus Christ, has been destroyed by death. Mary Magdalene is grief-stricken and she is shedding tears of sadness, crying in despair "They took my Master, and I don't know where they put him." Yet, when the Risen Jesus approaches her and asks, "Woman, why do you weep? Who are you looking for?" she does not recognize Him. Absorbed in her sorrow, and mistaking Him for the gardener, she replies, "Mister, if you took him, tell me where you put him so I can care for him."

Mary is convinced that this change means she no longer has anything to live for. It is only after Jesus speaks her name that Mary realizes Jesus is not dead; Jesus is alive! What Mary cherishes most has not been destroyed! In joy, she reaches out to touch her Lord and Master—to take hold and reassure herself that this is real, and not simply a dream. Jesus stops her, however, and says, "Don't cling to me, for I have not yet ascended to the Father." Jesus then instructs Mary to: "Go to my brothers and tell them, 'I ascend to my Father and your Father, my God and your God.'" This is Good News! But there is more to Jesus' message than the Good News of His ascension. There is the command to accept the fact of change.

"Don't cling to me," Jesus tells Mary. In essence, He is saying that He wants Mary to know that what He meant to her has not been lost, but it has changed. He must ascend to the Father so she must not cling to what He was. She must accept the new reality of who He is and His resurrection. Nothing essential has changed, but there are changes nevertheless, and she must accept these changes or she will lose all that is to be. Jesus shows us, unmistakably, that those things we value most, if they are worth valuing, persist through change. It is something that is not easily explainable. I recall a song from my childhood that begins:

> God gave Noah the rainbow sign,
> "No more water but fire next time."

It is a reminder that this earth will not stand forever. I am told that one day the sun, in its last stages of existence, will explode into a supernova and incinerate the earth and all that is in it. Gone will be the great works of Michelangelo. Gone will be DaVinci's *Mona Lisa* and his depiction of the Last Supper. The Taj Mahal, the Statue of Liberty, the Eiffel Tower, the London Bridge, the Pyramids and the Great Wall of China will be obliterated. Gone will be the music of Bach, Beethoven, Brahms, the Beatles, and Michael Jackson. The movies of Hitchcock, DeMille, and Spielberg; the novels of Dickens, Twain, and Clancy; the poems of Frost, Shelley, and Angelou; the works of Shakespeare, Plato, Aristotle, Luther, and yes, even the Bible, will be gone. Gone. They will all be gone.

Though many things we value will disappear, I believe that our highest and our best will be preserved. I believe it because that is what happened to Jesus. He died, but He was not destroyed. He lives today and is our highest value. And that ought to make us work to do our best, to give our best, to believe the best, and to seek to make a difference in the short time we are given.

Change. Change. Change.

Faith in God means relinquishing the old to prepare for the new: breaking eggs to make an omelet; giving up the caterpillar to see the butterfly; planting the seed to behold the rose. Faith in God means accepting new and more challenging responsibilities, even if we have only just figured out the previous ones. And it means watching our children prepare to take wings and leave for lives of their own. Paul was referring to this metamorphosis when he wrote to the church at Corinth (2 Cor. 5:17):

Now we look inside,
And what we see is that anyone united with the Messiah gets a fresh start,
Is created new.
The old life is gone; a new life burgeons!

"Time is filled with swift transition…
Build your hopes on things eternal,
Hold to God's unchanging hand."[1]

As we see the world change before us,
Technology rapidly moving throughout the world,
Space exploration boldly heading to places unknown,
Right before our eyes we witness
The change of our world.
And yet, we see poverty,
We see envy and strife,
We see racism, anger, violence, and the failure to forgive…
Some things seem to never change!

But…
Change my heart, O Lord, to see You,
An unchanging God who loves and cares for me!

"My hope is built on nothing less
Than Jesus' blood and righteousness…
On Christ the solid rock I stand,
All other ground is sinking sand!"[2]

Amen.

1. Jennie Wilson, "Hold to God's Unchanging Hand."
2. Edward Mote, "My Hope is Built on Nothing Less," circa 1834.

11

I Will Trust In The Lord, 'Til I Die!

God said this once and for all;
how many times have I heard it repeated?
"Strength comes straight from God."
(Ps. 62:11)

How does one reach the point where trust in God is a given? How do we reach a point when we can say with confidence that God is our rock, our sword and shield, and that nothing will shake our confidence in God? It is a simple thing to say how confident in God we are when things are going well for us. It is easy to affirm our faith when things are proceeding as planned. It is easy to speak with confidence when there aren't any challenges to our faith or obstacles in our way. But what about when we feel lost and want to give up? What about the times when we've been crying all night? Times when the road is rough and the going gets tough and the hills are hard to climb? Perhaps the psalmist has something to say to us in those moments.

The Psalms have been called the vehicle by which the Grace of Heaven comes to us with power to comfort and strengthen us. Psalms 60 through 62 grow out of the experience of an individual witnessing a crisis that has affected the entire nation. The Hebrews, who are at war with their enemies, believe that God has withdrawn the Divine hand from the army of the people. In Psalm 60, the desperate psalmist wails: "God! You walked off and left us, kicked our defenses to bits and stalked off angry." Psalm 60 ends with the psalmist crying out to God for help against a foe too difficult to defeat.

In Psalm 61:2 (NRSV), as the nation is in trouble, the psalmist speaks on its behalf, crying out that his soul is in distress. The psalmist tells us that he is lonely, afraid, pressed hard by troubles, and in need of protection and security:

O, God, from the end of the earth I call to you.

Where is the end of the earth? Perhaps it is that place people reach when they feel utterly alone. For some it is a place of sickness, sorrow, and sadness. For others it is a place of failure, frustration, and fear. Maybe the end of the earth is that place where African American slaves cried:

> Sometimes I feel like a motherless child,
> A long way from home.[1]

The end of the earth is that place where you are uneasy about the next step. It is the place where you feel you've reached the end of your rope. It is that place from where Jesus called out (Matt. 27:46):

> My God, my God, why have you forsaken me?

It is at this lonely and frightful place that the psalmist finds himself and the Nation of Israel. Yet, he still breathes a note of trust and confidence in God. He expresses hope in God's ability and willingness to help those who are faithful. The psalmist reminds us that the worst assaults on earth cannot diminish the greatness of the Lord who sits on high with resources we cannot imagine.

The psalmist has complete confidence in God. He shares that confidence with the people of Israel because he knows three important things.

God is our rock.

In times of trouble, when the storms of life are battering us from every front, each of us needs something immovable to sustain us. We need something, in spite of all that is going on around us, something that gives us the strength to sing the hymn of Edward Mote:

> On Christ the solid rock I stand,
> All other ground is sinking sand.

God is our fortress.

We all need a place to which we can retreat. A place of solitude. A sanctuary from the hustle and bustle of life. A shelter to protect us when the battle gets too heated. When the bullets fly too fast. When the kids are crying too loudly. When

---

1.   J. W. Johnson and J. R. Johnson, "Sometimes I feel like a Motherless Child," 1926.

the bills are coming too quickly. When trouble seems to be on every hand. In these moments, we need a fortress where we can re-collect our thoughts, redirect our hearts, reprogram our minds, and revive our souls.

God is our salvation.

It is when we do not know God that our fears overcome our hopes. It is when we seek salvation in those things that are not eternal that our lives become confused, discombobulated, and troubled.

The psalmist has learned to walk a path that depends on God and not himself…On God, and not his friends or his political choices…On God, and not his own intelligence or strength. The psalmist has learned to entrust his life, his problems, and his situation into the hands of the God of his salvation.

From Psalm 62:6–8, 11–12 (NRSV), hear again the words of the psalmist—words that are not just about his life, but about our lives also:

> For God alone my soul waits in silence.
> For my hope comes from the Lord.
> God alone is my rock and my salvation and my fortress
> I shall not be shaken.
> On God rests my deliverance and my honor;
> My mighty rock, my refuge, is God.
> Trust in God at all times, O people;
> Pour your heart out to the God of your refuge….
> Once God has spoken;
> Twice have I heard this:
> That power belongs to God;
> And that to thee, O God, belongs an everlasting love.

Lord,
We've placed our trust in things temporal,
We've placed our trust in the arms of flesh,
That fail us,
We've placed our trust in ourselves.
We have not called upon You to help us
In good times and in bad.

Let us enter into Your rest,
From the troubled experiences of our past,
The stumbling blocks of our present,
And the obstacles we place to our future.

Let us enter into Your safety,
From the anxiety of our hearts,
The confusion of our minds,
And the restlessness of our souls.

Let us rejoice in Your love
That destroys yokes of bondage,
That sets the captives free.
Lord, we lift Your name on high...

Amen.

12

The Power of Words

The Word was first, the Word present to God,
God present to the Word.
the Word was God,
in readiness for God from day one.
(John 1:1–2)

In *My Fair Lady,* Eliza Doolittle says to her two suitors:

> Words! Words! Words!
> Is that all you blighters can do?
> Don't talk of stars burning above;
> If you're in love, show me!

Now, those of us who are baptized believers ought to be concerned about this suspicion of words. After all, our faith is based on words. The Word of God, "…Thus says the Lord;" sermon words, prayer words: "Our Father, who art in heaven" hymn words:

> O, God our help in ages past,
> Our hope for years to come,
> Our shelter from the stormy blast
> And our eternal home.[1]

Where there is grief, we speak words of comfort, "…even when walking through death's dark valley, I will fear no evil" (Ps. 23:6). Where there is injustice, we use prophetic words:

> Truth forever on the scaffold,
> Wrong forever on the throne.

---

1.   Issac Watts, "Our God, Our Help in Ages Past,*"* 1719.

40

With that scaffold sways the future.
Behind the dim unknown stands God
Within the shadow keeping watch above his own.[2]

Where there is despair, we have words of hope. Where there is sickness, there are healing words. Where there is confusion, we bring words of peace. Where there is sin, we find words of salvation. And through Jesus Christ, the power of our words is returned to us. It is critical to understand that the words we speak can become words filled with grace and truth. It is significant to realize that our words can become instruments of redemption.

That is part of what the story of the demon Legion is about. What did Jesus do for the possessed man? He simply spoke words. We recall the story in the fifth chapter of Mark's Gospel (NRSV):

> Once in the area of the Gerasenes there was a man possessed with a multitude of personalities, a host of demons that called themselves Legion. Legion lived in a cemetery, chained to the tombstones and every so often broke away from his chains and ran through the town. On those occasions he was caught, taken back to the cemetery, bound, and chained again.

And what did Jesus do for this man? He didn't tell him to go wash in a pool. He didn't suggest he have more faith. Jesus didn't even lay hands on him to effect a healing. All Jesus did was speak words—simple words, just like you and I use every day.

The words Jesus spoke to the possessed man came in the form of a question: "What is your name?" Those words stopped the man in his tracks and forced him to respond to Jesus: "I am Legion, for we are many" (NRSV, Mark 5:9). Those words from Jesus were words this man had never heard before. Yes, people told him he was crazy. Others made it known that he was full of demons, and still others made it a point to let him know he was unacceptable in civilized society. But no one had ever spoken words of purpose to him. Jesus' words were full of grace and truth.

What Jesus offered this man is what He offers each of us: words of life and beauty. He offers us words that touch us where we hurt, and words that speak to us in places that doctors cannot reach. Jesus' words unlock our prisons and free us to be the people God has created us to be. The words that Jesus offers are still available to us today.

---

2.   James Russell Lowell, *The Present Crisis,* 1844.

The psalmist calls these words "a beam of light on my dark path" (Ps. 119:105). They are words that remind us of the God who so loved the world that Jesus was sent to save us from our sins. It is the Word of God that keeps, sustains, and strengthens us each and every day of our lives. Through the pain, heartaches, trouble, and challenges of our lives, God makes available to us the Divine, life-giving Word of love and hope.

"Blessed quietness,
Holy quietness,
What assurance in my soul...
On a stormy sea,
Speaking peace to me,
And the billows cease to roll..."[1]

Too often, O Lord,
I come before You with words...
Words of need, words of pain, words of desire...
Failing to realize that You offer to me
A way to enter into Your presence without restriction.
So I come before You in that holy quietness,
As You speak peace to me.
You speak peace in homes,
In communities,
In nations...

At Your word, You rebuke shame
And give joy to the oppressed...
Thank You for setting me free...

Amen.

1.   Manie P. Ferguson, "Blessed Quietness," circa 1897.

13

Awaken, To Life In God!

I came so they can have real and eternal life,
more and better life than they ever dreamed of.
(John 10:10)

Life is a game, and the games we play shape our lives and the world in which we live. Without games, we would languish in boredom. So it is not a question of "Shall we play a game?" but, rather, "What kind of game shall we play?"

I believe we are called to play the game of being awake to God and to each other. The game involves our receptiveness to the Word of God sown in our hearts as well as being open to the experience of this God of love and mystery. We have to bear in mind that human beings play other games that determine the way we see the world. These human games are deadly games. You know them: the race for money; the struggle for power; the competition for status. These games do not compare to the ultimate challenge—the game of being awake to each other, to the world around us, and to the God who made us and loves us.

We see this game of wakefulness in the Bible and in other religions. The prophets were awake to God. The Apostle Paul was awakened in a blinding light on the road to Damascus. Buddha was once asked:

> "Are you God?"
> He replied, "No."
> "Are you an angel, then?"
> "No," he said.
> "Then what are you?"
> Buddha replied, "I am awake."

When we are not awake, we become empty shells without connection to people or the world around us. When we are not awake, we *break* the connection between each other, ourselves, and our God.

Suicide is an attempt to remain asleep. Sometimes we seek the solace of sleep because it eases the pain and suffering that comes, at times, with the challenges of life. The consequences of being awake are serious. To be truly awake is to be like Abraham and Sarah, moving into a wilderness of uncharted, untried things.

When we are awake we no longer fear the unknown to the point that we choose to snooze rather than grow into new possibilities. When we are awake to the Word of God, we know it, and we understand how much we do *not* know about God and about life.

If we think that we know it all, there is no room left to experience the Divine Possibilities that come from the Eternal God of the Universe, who is full of surprises, gifts, and opportunities for us. So we must be open to the unknown. Open to twists and turns and confusion and to the satisfaction that comes from being awake to new ideas, new people, and new things.

Being awake teaches us how to deal with suffering instead of running from it. Being awake helps us to appreciate all creatures, great and small. Being awake helps us to recall our connection to each other and to God. If you can remain awake, you will experience the rewards of this game of life in laughter, love, hope, and in the mystery we call God.

Awake and sing
And let the heavenly joy bells ring
For the Lord is worthy to be praised, oh yes!
The Lord is worthy to be praised!

In the morning, Lord, when I arise...

I want to arise holy...
Set apart, consecrated for Your service,
Knowing who I am, because of who You are.

I want to arise aware...
Of Your beauty, of Your joy,
Of Your love that You demonstrated in Jesus Christ.

I want to arise ready...
To live for You, to battle against evil,
To promote justice, and to show mercy.

Awaken us, O God,
Show us where to go,
Breathe in us a spirit of love, peace, and joy...
Let there be a willingness to say Yes—
Yes to Your will,
Yes to Your love,
Yes to Your joy!

Amen.

14

What Does God Want?

But he's already made it plain how to live, what to do,
what God is looking for in men and women.
It's quite simple: Do what is fair and just to your neighbor,
be compassionate and loyal in your love,
and don't take yourself too seriously—
take God seriously.
(Mic. 6:8)

As a teenager and a young Christian, I was convinced above all else that what God wanted more than anything was for me to be in church. And I was there. I went to church every night. I went to church all day on Sundays. My focus on my place in church was steadfast. However, one night, while racing to get to church on time, I learned a valuable lesson about what God really wants.

I was making a mad dash for the subway on 135th street and Lenox Avenue, and I had to pass by a church that was under construction. As I passed under the scaffolding in front of the building, an elderly woman approached from the opposite side. As she made her feeble way towards me, she began to fall. I reached out to catch her and managed to keep her head from hitting the ground. Believing that if I stayed any longer I would miss the train that would get me to church on time, I continued my sprint for the subway. The drive to be in church—worshiping God and carrying out all of my required religious rituals—was deeply embedded, so I left that woman lying on the ground despite her need for further assistance. I continued on my way to church, certain that God wanted me there.

We often misunderstand what God wants. The Hebrew people encountered the same dilemma. In chapter six of the Book of Micah, the prophet tells us of a dispute between God and Israel:

"Dear people, how have I done you wrong, Have I burdened you, worn you out? Answer!" God asks the Hebrews. "I delivered you from a bad life in Egypt; I paid a good price to get you out of slavery. I sent Moses to lead you—and Aaron

47

and Miriam to boot! Remember what Balak king of Moab tried to pull, and how Balaam son of Beor turned the tables on him.

Remember all those stories about Shittim and Gilgal…."

The people respond, "How can I stand up before God and show proper respect to the high God? Should I bring an armload of offerings topped off with yearling calves? Would God be impressed with thousands of rams, with buckets and barrels of olive oil? Would he be moved if I sacrificed my firstborn child, my precious baby, to cancel my sin?" In other words, the nation of Israel is asking, just as we might ask on any trying day of our lives: God, what do you want? I've done everything, why isn't it enough?

In Micah 6:8, God offers a clear answer: "Do what is fair and just to your neighbor, be compassionate and loyal in your love, and don't take yourself too seriously, take God seriously."

Now, it is not always easy to know exactly what loving one another entails, or to know what God wants us to do in every situation. What we do know is that hate, war, violence, revenge and all of the other means through which the world gets what it wants are not options for people of faith. What God wants is for us to love one another. In fact, Jesus tells us we are *commanded* to love one another. We live under a commandment to love and to do so without thought to personal benefit; a commandment to love selflessly. Jesus says: "This is my command: Love one another the way I loved you. This is the very best way to love. Put your life on the line for your friends. You are my friends when you do the things I command you" (John 15:12).

God calls us to live meaningful lives, to be fair and compassionate, and to take God seriously! When we uphold the commandment to love, we please the Lord, our God, who turns our values upside down and inside out, and delivers meaning to our lives.

"There's not a friend like the lowly Jesus,
No, not one! No, not one!...

Jesus knows all about our struggles;
He will guide until the day is done;
There's not a friend like the lowly Jesus,
No, not one! No, not one!"[1]

Lord, I fail to acknowledge the friendship
You've given to me in Christ.
When I come before You asking for things I want,
You remind me of what You want from me.

So, Lord, I give You this day,
But I know it is not enough!
O Lord, I give You all that I own,
But I know it is not enough!
O Lord, I give You my time and my gifts,
But I know they are not enough!
So I give You my soul
And I surrender to You,
Who is greater than I can ever be.
Help me to be more like You!

In Jesus' name,
Amen.

---

1.   Johnson Oatman, Jr., "There's Not a Friend Like the Lowly Jesus," 1895.

15

Secrets

Don't be intimidated. Eventually everything is going to be out in the open, and everyone will know how things really are. So don't hesitate to go public now.
(Matt. 10:26–27)

What is so intriguing about secrets? Why do millions of readers buy books and magazines that discuss the secret lives of the rich and famous? Certainly part of the attraction is the mystery of it all, and the desire to penetrate into the unknown. But another aspect is that secrets have power, and the sharing of secrets is the transference of power.

Some secrets are better left private, but many secrets ought to be revealed. Jesus reminds us that true liberation comes when our inner struggles can be shared with others. Too much damage in our society is often wrought through secrets—child abuse and the fear of revelation; spousal abuse and the shame it brings; drug and alcohol addiction and the attempt to hide it from others.

There is healing in the revelation of secrets. When we can find support groups and Christian fellowships where we feel the freedom to share our secrets with others who listen, understand, and accept us, then we experience God in our lives with one another.

Sometimes we may discover secrets in life that are enriching and empowering because they bind us to other people in a special way. After reading the scripture where Jesus says, "Eventually everything is going to be out in the open, and everyone will know how things really are," we wonder about those areas of our lives that we want guarded and kept private from others. But the reality is that God knows us, sees us, and understands us, and from this all-knowing God there is no escape. This is why we pray: "Almighty God, to whom all hearts are open, and all desires known, and from whom no secrets are hidden…"

That's a little bit scary, isn't it? God knows things about us that we would rather *no one* know. There are moments when we may want to escape from this all-knowing God. The psalmist put it this way (Ps. 139:7–12):

> Is there anyplace I can go to avoid your spirit?
>> To be out of your sight?
> If I climb to the sky, you're there!
>> If I go underground, you're there!
> If I flew on morning's wings
>> To the far western horizon
> You'd find me in a minute—
>> You're already there waiting!
> Then I said to myself, "Oh, God even sees me in the dark!
>> At night I'm immersed in the light!"
> It's a fact, darkness isn't dark to you;
>> Night and day, darkness and light, they're all the same to you!

There is no eluding God. God knows all about us and yet, with amazing grace, God accepts and understands us. Our God knows us better than we know ourselves. God allows us to approach the Divine altar in secret and abide under the Almighty shadow. Yes, God respects our secrets, strengthens us, and helps us face the hidden places of our lives. God allows us to share our secrets so that we might be made whole to serve the Divine will and purpose.

Lord,
Often we are afraid of the truth
Because we hold on to our secrets...
We have not completely confessed to You
All the thoughts of our hearts.
We've covered the guilt and hid the shame.
We mask ourselves before You and others.
Rebuke the devil in our minds,
Take away our shame.

Liberate us to speak to You,
And bring us into fellowship
With all the hurting people
Who are growing in the faith
Of our Lord Jesus Christ.

Amen.

16

God's Business

The next day they found him in the Temple seated among the teachers,
listening to them and asking questions.
The teachers were all quite taken with him,
impressed with the sharpness of his answers.
(Luke 2:46–47)

How we deal with people on a daily basis says much about us. It says who we are, what we believe, and what is important to us. Are we good listeners? Are we worth listening to? Are we opinionated? Is there consistency between what we say and what we do?

Our daily encounters with others reveal much about us as individuals. Likewise, we can learn much about the life and teachings of Jesus by taking a closer look at the encounters He had with people during His ministry.

Jesus' first recorded encounter is with the teachers in the temple and His own parents, while traveling to Jerusalem for the Passover feast. The feast had ended, and it was time to return home. But Jesus, marching to a different drummer, stayed behind in Jerusalem, without informing His parents.

The issue was not disrespect for His parents, but rather, respect for the temple and its importance to the faith. We know that Jesus revered this institution because He made it a point to be there at the appointed times. Scripture tells us that He spoke from the temple's pulpit, supported its rituals and traditions, and sought to understand its mission and purpose.

We also know that, even at this early age, Jesus was a marvel. He was a theologian without theological training. He was a scholar without a scholarly education. He was able to discuss with those learned men the whys and wherefores of their profession and to astound them with the depth of His insight and understanding. Not bad for a 12-year-old kid!

When His parents returned to Jerusalem seeking him, after going a day's journey out of the way, they find Him sitting among the teachers, listening to them, and asking questions. When His parents confront Him about His "disrespectful" behavior, Jesus responds, "Why were you looking for me? Didn't you know that I had to be here, dealing with the things of my Father?" (Luke 2:49)

I think you and I should always be mindful of what God's business is about. It is *not* about money or material gain. It is *not* about fame or fortune. It is *not* concerned with status or rank. It is *not* focused on promotions, perks, or privileges. God's business is to *seek and to save the lost.* As Jesus came to remind us in Luke 4:18–19, God's business is also:

> ...to preach the Message of good news to
> the poor,
> ...to announce pardon to prisoners and
> recovery of sight to the blind,
> To set the burdened and battered free,
> to announce, "This is God's year to act!"

For Jesus, God's business was about a lonely woman on her way to a well to draw water; it was about five thousand followers hungry to have their souls fed by the Living Word; it was about a blind man who wanted to see again; and it was about a leper who wanted to be healed and allowed back into the community. Jesus, who understood God's business, decided not to leave it to our imaginations. Instead, He offered clear direction as to what God's business is about, and how it reveals itself in our lives.

As people of faith and followers of Christ, God's business is our business. It is our responsibility, to God and to each other, to love one another as God loves us. We teach God's care and concern when we care for others. We demonstrate God's love for people by how we love others. We teach tolerance by being tolerant; patience by being patient; acceptance by accepting others.

May each of us strive to be the kind of person that Jesus was here on earth. As He acted in the temple, let us, despite our daily difficulties, devote *our* lives towards the fulfillment of God's business.

God,
Your business is about souls…
The soul that is hurting and grieving
From the loss of loved ones…
The soul that is troubled and seeking
For meaning and purpose…
The soul that has broken fellowship with You.

Help us prioritize the day,
So that we can seize it for You.
Give us the spirit of repentance,
For being so individualistic,
Concerned only about ourselves,
That we forgot the business that You are in…
Reaching the lost, the wounded, the oppressed,
The molested, the battered, the abused, the sinner.
Give us the spirit of hope,
That the warfare we fight is not carnal,
But mighty in You!

Make us truth-tellers, justice shapers, love spreaders,
In the business of the Gospel…

We pray in Jesus' name,
Amen.

17

Even So, Lord Jesus, Come!

This very Jesus who was taken up from among you to heaven
will come as certainly—and mysteriously—as he left.
(Acts 1:11)

One thing is certain about the early Christian church: they believed that Jesus was coming back again. Over and over in the New Testament it is clear that there was a conviction that this Jesus who had been taken away would return. The Apostle Paul said Jesus would descend from on high. The Book of Revelation 1:7 declares, "Yes, he's on his way! Riding the clouds, he'll be seen by every eye...."

For the early Christians, the Second Coming was a hope that loomed larger than life itself. It called them to look beyond the limitations of this human existence and be transformed by the creative and redemptive power of God at work through Jesus Christ.

It is unfortunate that for many of us, this hope has become a small part of life. We do not hold our breath waiting for Jesus to return. People today simply do not give much thought to the return of Jesus Christ. In a survey, when people were asked, "Do you believe Jesus is coming again?" people responded: "I don't care," "Are you kidding?" and even, "I hope he gets back before my test on Friday."

But the news of Christ's return was Good News to the disciples. It gave comfort to the troubled and weary. It offered peace to those confused about life. It caused people to radically alter their lives. Missionaries left their homes to declare this Good News. Teachers left their countries to open schools in faraway lands.

John Newton was a man who could be considered the lowest form of human being. He made millions of dollars peddling the flesh of other human beings, in what we know as the slave trade. Yet Newton became so enamored with this Good News regarding Christ's return that he freed all of his slaves, gave away his millions, and began spreading the news of this King who was coming soon. Later,

Newton would write perhaps the best-known and most beloved hymn of the Christian faith:

> Amazing grace, how sweet the sound
> That saved a worm like me.
> I once was lost, but now I'm found,
> Was blind, but now I see.

As Christians, we must live our lives watching and waiting for Jesus Christ to return. The question for us is: how do we do this? Does it mean we turn our backs on this life and this world? Do we sell all we have and head for the temple in Jerusalem? Not quite. It means that wherever we are, in whatever we do, in each deed we perform, we must live our lives believing that each moment may be the last. We must allow God to claim us, and live our lives—every second—to the glory of God.

Jesus tells us to live our lives in anticipation of His return. For those who do, there is no guessing about why we are here. There is no need to search to find the meaning of life. Our lives are formed and our directions are given as we live faithfully, waiting and watching for the coming of our Savior Jesus Christ.

Lord,
We have beckoned for You to come,
We have sent out the call for Your arrival.
But we have not done what You told us to do…

To make disciples
To clothe the naked
To feed the hungry
To heal the sick
To raise the dead

We have not waited for You with a sense of urgency
And so we've been idle,
Envious of one another—
Fault finders, criticizers, betrayers.

Help us to do what You told us to do,
So when that day comes
And we all see Jesus…
What a day of rejoicing that will be!

Amen.

18

My Soul Looks Back and Wonders...How I Got Over

We may be immersed in tears, yet always filled with deep joy;
living on handouts, yet enriching many;
having nothing, having it all.
(2 Cor. 6:10)

As Christians, we must seek constantly to reflect on where our devotions lie. Which material things engulf us, engross us, and keep us from relating to God as we ought? We are challenged to get moving in our lives—to move, grow, develop, and be willing to listen and to hear all that is taking place around us. We ought to develop a sense of what is important in our lives:

To be able to hear the cry of a newborn baby and the cries of those who are suffering from broken hearts, broken homes, and shattered dreams;

To reach out to those whose will to live has been destroyed by disease or poverty;

To pay attention to the poor and those who are hurting, helpless, and hopeless;

To be willing to get our lives right with God and to seek forgiveness from the God who is our Savior;

To be willing to sacrifice something for what has been given to us and to realize how much we have received from our ancestors, from our nation, and most of all from our God, who sacrificed Jesus that we might live;

To remember we are dust, and it is to dust we must return;

And to be thankful God doesn't make just any old kind of dust. God makes dust so important that Jesus was sent to suffer on the cross and die for it—to die for us. That makes us unique.

We must seek to affirm life, especially our own. It is time to connect our lives with the deep rhythms of living as we feast and fast and live and die. Hear the words of the Apostle Paul (2 Cor. 6:1–13):

> Companions as we are in this work with you, we beg you,
> Please don't squander one bit
> Of this marvelous life God has given us…
> With pure heart, clear head, steady hand;
> In gentleness, holiness, and honest love;
> When we're telling the truth,
> And when God is showing his power;
> When we're doing out best setting things right;
> When we're praised, and when we're blamed;
> Slandered, and honored;
> True to our word, though distrusted;
> Ignored by the world, but recognized by God;
> Terrifically alive, though rumored to be dead;
> Beaten within an inch of our lives,
> But refusing to die;
> Immersed in tears,
> Yet always filled with deep joy;
> Living on handouts, yet enriching many;
> Having nothing, having it all.
> Dear, Dear Corinthians, I can't tell you how much
> I long for you to enter this wide-open spacious life.
> We didn't fence you in. The smallness you feel comes from within you.
> Your lives aren't small, but you're living them in a small way.
> I'm speaking as plainly as I can and with great affection.
> Open up your lives. Live openly and expansively!

Today, I want to invite you to imagine your own beginning—the very beginning. Imagine your conception, and your growth in your mother's womb. Think about how far you have come since that time. Then take a moment to think about where God is taking you from *this* moment forward and keep in mind that:

We serve a mighty wonderful God!

Give me the strength to take one day at a time.
To have peace about what I cannot do,
Courage to do what I can do.

Let not the past blur my present, or stifle my future.
Let me look back and see You there all the time.
Let me look now and witness Your presence.
Help me to look beyond what I cannot see,
Cannot taste, cannot hear, cannot smell...
And help me to sense Your presence.

Open my heart, dear Lord,
Help me to see where You brought me from...
A mighty long way!
Wonderful Jesus!
Wonderful Lord!

Your grace has sustained me,
Your mercy is everlasting.
Let Your mighty hand mold and shape
This vessel of clay.

Amen.

19

The True Light

The Word became flesh and blood,
…Generous inside and out, true from start to finish.
(John 1:14)

When tragedy strikes we often want to know *why?* What happened, and why did it happen? Answering the "why" question incorrectly can lead to a loss of faith.

I worked as a teenager in the New York Public Library. I often took opportunities to share my faith with my co-workers and others I met. One day I spoke to a co-worker who was sitting by herself, in tears. When I inquired about her concerns, she shared them with me. When I offered to pray with her, she responded: "I have had no place in my life for God and religion." I asked her why, and she said that once, when she was going through a particularly difficult time, she turned to the Lord and asked, "Why? When will my troubles cease?" She felt that God was unresponsive and indifferent, convincing her that she was on her own and could not rely on God to take care of her.

The early Christians often experienced tough and testing times. Many were originally Jews, but their "radical" beliefs resulted in their expulsion from the synagogue. The Roman authority persecuted them for their faith, and some of them were put to death for their beliefs. So when they gathered for worship and devotions, there was a deep need in their lives for the Good News. Whenever conflicts arose, or one of them was killed for his/her beliefs, they would read the first few verses of John's Gospel for encouragement:

> The Word was first,
> the Word present to God,
> God present to the Word.
> The Word was God,
> in readiness for God from day one.

Everything was created through him;
nothing—not one thing!—
came into being without him.
What came into existence was Life,
and the Life was Light to live by.
The Life-Light blazed out of the darkness;
the darkness couldn't put it out.

For the early Christians—those troubled souls!—these verses recalled the words of Genesis, reminding them that in the beginning, it was God who created the heavens and the earth. It was God who gave the earth its shape and form. It was the Eternal God of the Universe who breathed life into its existence. And now Jesus, the Eternal Word who had been with God in the beginning, and who Himself was God, was with them also.

Sometimes the suffering and persecution of these Christians made them feel lifeless. Sometimes their world was shrouded in the darkness of evil and persecution. But Jesus brought light into their world. Jesus was the fulfillment of the hopes and expectations of that baptizing preacher named John, to whom their parents had flocked to hear in the wilderness. And these early Christians believed that Jesus could fulfill their own hopes and expectations as well, and that He could—and *would*—give them a new beginning for their lives.

So in the moments of our lives when we feel broken, inadequate, discouraged, despondent, and defeated; when our faith seems to fail us, and the presence of evil seems to surround us, we hear the Scriptures and we are reminded of the early Christians' belief that God is a God of new beginnings.

When people we love and respect die, or when they suffer, we often wonder *why?* The scripture of John 1:9–14 reminds us:

The Life-Light was the real thing:
Every person entering Life
he brings into Light.
He was in the world,
the world was there through Him,
and yet the world didn't even notice.
He came to His own people,
but they didn't want Him.
But whoever did want Him,
who believed He was who He claimed
and would do what He said,

He made to be their true selves,
their child-of-God selves.
These are the God-begotten,
not blood-begotten,
not flesh-begotten,
not sex-begotten.
The Word became flesh and blood,
and moved into the neighborhood.
We saw the glory with our own eyes,
the one-of-a-kind glory,
like Father, like Son,
Generous inside and out,
true from start to finish.

The same God who gave us life can turn our lives around. The God who sent life into the world through Jesus Christ can also shed light on the darkness that sometimes seems to overwhelm us.

Let us look this day to the God of new beginnings, in whom we live and breathe and have our being.

"Why should I feel discouraged?
...Why should my heart feel lonely?
...When Jesus is my fortress,
A constant friend is He,
His eye is on the sparrow,
And I know He watches me!"[1]

Thank You, Lord, for the light of Your love...
Your light, penetrating the darkest hour,
Your light, shining in the most horrific situations,
Your light, breaking through
The darkest night of the soul.

Thank You, Lord, for reminding me that
You always are looking for me...
And You find me in some of the most awkward places,
In some of the most vulnerable situations,
You find me lifeless, useless, and pitiful,
You find me as a sinner!
I know You watch over me!

"I sing because I'm happy!
I sing because I'm free!"

Thank You, Lord!
Amen.

---

1.   Civilla D. Martin, "His Eye is on the Sparrow," 1905.

20

Choose Life!

I call Heaven and Earth to witness against you today:
I place before you Life and Death, Blessing and Curse.
Choose life so that you and your children will live.
(Deut. 30:19)

In the Book of Deuteronomy, Moses' words are as sharp as a surgeon's scalpel as he cuts to the heart of the matter. He reminds the people of God's steadfast love. He reminds the people that God is with them. They can see God in the cloud that leads them by day and the pillar of fire that guides them by night.

While standing on the edge of the Promised Land, Moses gives his farewell address. He tries to remind the people of what God has brought them through and what God is leading them towards. And then with passion and clarity, Moses declares: "I call Heaven and Earth to witness against you today: I place before you Life and Death, Blessing and Curse. Choose life so that you and your children will live."

Given the opportunity to choose between God and Satan and good and evil, there is no question we would choose God and good, right? But too often, when we walk into the supermarket of life, we do *not* choose God and good, do we? No! Do we choose God and good when we choose to treat people as intruders in our lives and in our work? No! When we choose to treat people as less than human, are we choosing God and good? No! And we are also not making a choice for God and good when we choose to hate those who are different from us.

And unfortunately, our choices are not always clear and sharp. Sometimes we must choose despite thick fog, muddy issues, dim light.

In a play by Henrik Ibsen, the curtain opens and a spotlight shines in the middle of the stage. A lone man walks around the light several times. A police officer happens to pass by, and he asks the man if there's a problem. The man says, "I've lost my watch." So the police officer joins the search. After a few minutes the police officer says, "Are you sure you lost it here?" "Oh, no," says the man, "I lost it over there." "So why are we searching here?" the police officer asks. "Well," the man answers, "there's no light over there!"

Sometimes we must make decisions, and the choices are not obvious. So what do we do when choices are not simple? How do we make decisions in the face of uncertainty?

First of all, we acknowledge that we cannot see clearly. The Apostle Paul said that we "don't yet see things clearly. We're squinting in a fog, peering through a mist" (1 Cor. 13:12). That is to say, we are finite human beings with limited ability to know all there is to know.

Secondly, we make our best choice on the basis of the best information and perspective we have at the time. Sometimes the most we can do is to make the choice that is closest to what we believe demonstrates God's love for us and our love for God. This might require that we take a close walk with God in order to nurture our faith. Our time spent in devotions, reading our Bibles, or on our knees in prayer, ought to sensitize us to those moments when we *aren't* on our knees, or reading our Bibles, or gathered in fellowship. At those times we need to listen for the Divine Voice, leading us to make the right decisions.

Thirdly, we need to be sensitive about our choices, especially during times when our decisions affect others and may even hurt them. We must also be aware of moments when our decisions *have* hurt others. We should be willing to admit our mistakes to God and seek the forgiveness of those whom we have hurt. Remember: it is not what *others think of you* that prevents you from having a right relationship with God, but rather what *you* think of *others*!

Finally, we should remember that God is with us. That is the point of the Deuteronomy text: God hangs in there. God cleaves to us. God walks with us, talks with us, and claims us as God's own. Even when we make choices that send us into a wilderness to wander (God only knows for how long!), God sends a pillar of fire to remind us of the Divine presence. God's presence allows us to live with hope for tomorrow, and it allows us to cope in the face of uncertainty. God's presence gives us strength for today, and the ability to make choices for our lives, and for the lives of those we love.

Our choices must reflect our relationship with God. Our choices should help those who need to know and experience the Divine. By what emanates from us, others should be drawn to God. In choosing God, we choose life and all that God has promised.

God,
We pray today that You will help us
As we journey through life.
Teach us to make right choices for our lives,
Choices that reflect our relationship with You.

This we ask in Your most holy Name,
Amen.

21

What Now?

Later on that day, the disciples had gathered together, but, fearful of the Jews, had locked all the doors in the house. Jesus entered, stood among them, and said, "Peace to you." Then he showed them his hands and side. The disciples, seeing the Master with their own eyes, were exuberant. Jesus repeated his greeting: "Peace to you. Just as the Father sent me, I send you." Then he took a deep breath and breathed into them. "Receive the Holy Spirit," he said.
(John 20:19–22)

The Gospel of John is called the Gospel of Belief because it is written for both believers and unbelievers so that all might receive eternal life. John's Gospel is filled with stories of great faith and of deep doubt overcome. John shares stories about faith that is weak and shallow, and faith that is strong and deep.

In John 20, it is the evening following Resurrection Morning, a testing time for the disciples of Jesus Christ. They are in the midst of chaos, confusion, doubt, and despair. We have all experienced times such as these—testing times when something has happened in our lives that we are left perplexed by the event, unsure of ourselves and fearful about what is to come. Our faith and confidence are shaken to the core. We are left with that perennial question: *What do we do now?*

In Sondheim's musical play *Into the Woods,* a narrator leads us through a medley of various fairy tales. The narrator tells the audience of Little Red Riding Hood making her way into the woods to visit Grandma. We hear the story of Jack and the beanstalk, as Jack goes into the woods to sell his cow. There's Cinderella dressed in her finest gown, riding in a pumpkin carriage as she goes into the woods on her way to the ball, and Rapunzel with her long hair, stuck in a tower in the woods.

The narrator describes Jack climbing the beanstalk and causing the death of the Giant. Then the Giant's wife demands that one of the many characters be sacrificed in return for the death of her husband. Unable to choose among themselves, the characters come out of the play, grab the narrator, and feed him to the Giant's wife. There is just one problem: *What do they do now?*

None of them knows the rest of the play, and so they look at one another, asking "What do we do now? Who will lead us through the rest of the story?"

In the Gospel of John, the disciples are struggling with the same questions. Jesus had been crucified, and with His death the disciples lost the assurance that all was right. They had watched in fear as the Roman soldiers led Jesus away from Gethsemane. They had stood by in fear while Jesus went through the mockery of a trial. They had run away in fear while He suffered on the cross. Fear told them that at any moment, the soldiers would come and carry them off to their *own* trials and executions. Now they are huddled together in fear, locked behind closed doors in an unknown house, at an unspecified location, wondering: *What do we do now?*

Jesus answers this question Himself. He appears to His disciples and calms their fears with the words "Peace to you."

Has fear ever gripped your life, sent you into hiding, shut you down emotionally, and made you unable to respond or communicate? Franklin Roosevelt was onto something when he declared, "The only thing we have to fear is fear itself." Fear is a paralyzing emotion. It stifles our ability to stand up for justice and against oppression. Fear keeps us from moving ahead, and it hinders our ability to make decisions about our lives.

Nothing happens when you are afraid. That commitment to a partner is put off if you are afraid it will never work. Those plans to begin a business are put on hold if you are afraid that it might fail. College is delayed if you fear that you will not succeed. Nothing happens when we live in fear.

And so Jesus greets His disciples after He is raised from the dead, and He calms their fears. Jesus must calm their fears so that He can challenge their faith. He is ready to enlist His disciples for the work of the ministry. He does not simply give them a mission, but He *commissions* them, in much the same way that a commander-in-chief commissions officers. He gives them the authority to carry out the ministry. Jesus breathes on them and gives them new life, just as God breathed a new humanity into being in that first creation. Sometimes we need the Holy Spirit to breathe on us and challenge our faith so that we can continue the work for which He was sent. The challenge is to have faith that God is in control.

So what do we do now? We remember that, according to the Book of Hebrews, "faith, is the firm foundation under everything that makes life worth living. It's our handle on what we can't see" (Heb. 11:1). Faith tells us to believe that although there may continue to be wars and rumors of wars, people will one day "turn their swords into shovels, their spears into hoes. No more will nation fight nation; they won't play war anymore," and there will be peace in the land (Isa. 2:4). Faith tells us to stay the course and fight the good fight. Eventually we will all reach the place "where the wicked no longer trouble anyone and bone-weary people get a long-deserved rest" (Job 3:17). We will continue to trust and continue to believe. We will maintain our faith, remembering that Jesus said, in Matthew 28:20:

> I'll be with you as you do this, day after day after day,
> right up to the end of the age.

Breathe on me Lord,
breathe on me.

Let the breath of the Lord
now breathe on me.

Renew my faith and restore my joy in You.
Give me strength to move forward in my life
That I might serve You
With all my heart, mind and soul.

I ask this because I know You hear
Our faintest cries.

Amen.

22

All We Need

The Lord is my shepherd, I shall not want.
(NIV, Ps. 23:1)

Dave Carey, a retired Navy captain, was a prisoner of war in Vietnam. At an annual meeting of the Military Chaplains Association almost thirty years after his release, Carey said:

> To survive the torture…brutality…and the dehumanization of our imprisonment and to combat the gnawing fears of dishonoring our country, of never seeing our loved ones again…while battling depression, and with the enemy threatening death, we formulated a mission statement…a declaration of faith we hoped would see us through.

He said the mission statement wasn't long or complicated, but it was both simple and hopeful, and it was just three words: *Return with honor.*

Dave Carey went on to say that if he wished anything during his imprisonment, it was that he knew more scripture from the Bible, but he did not. And so he quoted to himself daily the only scripture he knew—the 23rd Psalm of David (NIV).

The Lord is my shepherd, I shall not be in want.
He makes me lie down in green pastures,
He leads me beside quiet waters,
He restores my soul.
He guides me in paths of righteousness
for his name's sake.
Even though I walk
through the valley of the shadow of death,
I will fear no evil,

for you are with me;
your rod and your staff,
they comfort me.
You prepare a table before me
in the presence of my enemies.
You anoint my head with oil;
my cup overflows.
Surely goodness and love will follow me
all the days of my life,
and I will dwell in the house of the Lord
forever.

Psalm 23 is David's declaration of faith and trust in God, and a reminder for us that God is the only thing we need. Do we really believe that God is the only need in our lives? Some of us believe we need luck, not God. Luck would at least win us the lottery. Some of us believe we need health- and life-insurance more than we need God. All too often, God takes a back seat to the things we think we need in order to be safe and secure: money, weapons, power, success, a bigger house, a promotion, perfect children, perfect relationships. These are things that we hope will make us feel more secure about ourselves and our lives, despite the uncertainties and challenges of life.

Look at David. Somehow, through the uncertainties and challenges of his life, David discovers the importance of an attachment to something greater than himself. He finds something eternal: God. David experiences, like a sheep with a good shepherd, the love and care of a faithful God.

What, you might ask, *does the psalmist know about the 21st century?* What does this psalmist know about our lack of satisfaction with life, about our struggles with addictions, pain, divorce, loneliness, aging, and all of the other afflictions that plague us today? What does the psalmist know about our lives and the uncertainties and challenges we face every day? It is easy to assume that the centuries between the psalmist and ourselves obstruct the possibility for mutual understanding.

But David does know about our experiences and sufferings. Psalm 23 is what is called a *todah* (a Hebrew word, meaning that the psalmist is very close to the experience about which he is writing). Now, we do not know which experience David is close to at the moment he is writing this psalm. Is it a military ambush, a rape in his family, his own rebellion against God, or imminent death? Whatever the occasion for this *todah* called Psalm 23, David chooses to testify—not about the challenges in his life, but about the confidence he has in God.

How can we cope with the ugliness of life? How do we bear the burdens of our past and the uncertainties of tomorrow? The 23rd Psalm gives us an answer. It is a God-honored way to give witness to the good and faithful God who is our Lord and Shepherd. When our trust is betrayed, when our friends lie to us, when our enemies surround us to do us harm, we need to hear and know that what we have in God is greater than what we lack in life—the God who is our Shepherd, and who cares and provides for us.

Dear God,
I am confident that
Through all of the challenges of my life,
You will see me through.

Grant me wisdom, and courage
For the living of these days.

Give me the assurance
Of Your abiding love and trust
And give me the strength
To give my love and trust to You.

I pray this in faith.
Amen.

23

What God Thinks

The mystery is that people who have never heard of God and those who have heard of him all their lives (what I've been calling outsiders and insiders) stand on the same ground before God. They get the same offer, same help, same promises in Christ Jesus. The Message is accessible and welcoming to everyone, across the board.
(Eph. 3:4–6)

Return to Me is a movie that tells the story of Rob, whose wife Elizabeth is killed tragically in a car crash. Rob decides to donate his wife's heart to someone in need of a heart transplant. The woman who receives the heart transplant, Grace, writes an anonymous letter of thanks to her unknown benefactor for the gift of her new heart and life. A year or so later, unaware of their medical connection, Rob and Grace meet, become friends, and fall in love. On a visit to Rob's home, Grace discovers the thank you letter she had written following her surgery. The realization that the heart of Rob's dead wife is now beating in her body sends Grace running in anguish to the home of a friend, crying: "What was God thinking?"

Have you ever wondered what God thinks? For example, what was God thinking when God created the duckbill platypus—a furry mammal, with a duck's bill, that lays eggs? Or what was God thinking by allowing the cockroach to evolve into a virtually indestructible insect? The poet Ogden Nash, voicing the human frustration with the thoughts of this omniscient God penned these words:

> The Lord in heaven made the fly
> and then forgot to tell us why.

Surely you've wondered what God was thinking when God created us—male, female; red, yellow, black, white, brown; gay, straight—and then ordered us to live on this terrestrial ball in peace and harmony with respect and love for one another?

The Book of Ephesians speaks to us about questions, mysteries, secrets and what God thinks. The Apostle Paul tells the Ephesians what God thinks. He breaks away from his religious terrorism against Christians and his cultural dogmatism to bring the Good News of God's love through Jesus Christ. While the other apostles remain culturally exclusive and confine their preaching and teaching to building what would have been a wonderful faith among Jews, Paul forges a new faith—*a new humanity*—under God that is "welcoming to everyone, across the board" (Eph. 3:6). Paul tells us that the mystery of what God thinks "has been made clear by God's Spirit" and calls upon us to have respect for all (Eph. 3:5).

Moreover, in unveiling the "mystery of faith," Paul reveals the gift of God's amazing Grace. Indeed, God's Grace can be described as nothing *less than* amazing. God's Grace speaks to us of the love of Jesus Christ, and the power of the Holy Spirit.

In this epistle we get a glimpse of God's thinking from the beginning of time, which is not a mystery at all, Paul tells us. The apostle explains that God's thinking is an act of unconditional love. Paul reminds us in his letter to the Ephesians that the answers to our questions are not clouded in mystery, but are made open and plain by the God who created us all (Eph. 3:9).

God blessed me with a profound insight into the nature of Divine thought when I first encountered the person who was to become my wife. I was two months into the start of my naval career when I met Nereida. It was a Saturday afternoon and I was walking through the Orange Park Mall in Jacksonville, Florida. An acquaintance, who happened to be a fellow naval officer, spotted me in the mall and said, "Bernard, I want you to meet one of the new nurses recently assigned to the naval hospital."

Now I was thinking that I was simply meeting a new shipmate, or maybe even a new friend, but God was thinking that I was meeting the person destined to become my wife and the mother of our two wonderful sons! God tells us in the Book of Isaiah, chapter 55, verse 8, "I don't think the way you think. The way you work isn't the way I work."

Jesus helps us to understand the difference between our thinking and Divine thinking.

For example, we think that if someone has judged us unfairly they are responsible for coming to us and seeking reconciliation, but God thinks:

> If you enter your place of worship…to make an offering, [and] you suddenly remember a grudge a friend has against you, abandon your offering, leave immediately, go to this friend and make things right. Then and only then, come back and work things out with God. (Matt. 5:23–24)

You might think it is okay to love your neighbors and hate your enemies, but God thinks that you should:

> …love your enemies. Let them bring out the best in you, not the worst. When someone gives you a hard time, respond with the energies of prayer, for then you are working out of your true selves, your God-created selves. This is what God does. (Matt. 5:43–44).

You and I must remember these words of God: "I don't think the way you think. The way you work isn't the way I work." We can't know *all* that God is thinking. But we can be certain that God thinks of us. Without regard to our status, color, gender, or the religion we follow, God thinks of us! No matter what trials and tribulations we may face, no matter how challenging the times may be, God thinks of us! Yesterday God thought of us. Today God thinks of us. Tomorrow and forever more, God will think of us.

This is the God who has done nothing but think of us ever since our separation in the Garden of Eden. If you want to know what God is thinking, it isn't a secret or a mystery. It isn't privileged communication or top-secret information that requires a code to crack;

God thinks of us!

God,
You are the source of all that is good in our lives.
It is so easy to allow the challenges of our lives
To make us feel far from You.

Help us to know each and every day
That You walk with us,
Talk with us
And sustain us.

Thank You, God, for Your love,
Grace, and mercy.
Amen.

~

Yesterday, today, forever
Jesus is the same.
All may change but Jesus never,
Glory to His name.[1]

1.   Albert B. Simpson, "Yesterday, Today, Forever," 1890.

24

Remaining Faithful and Obedient

Don't bother your head with braggarts or wish you could succeed like the wicked.
(Ps. 37:1)

During the tryouts for *American Idol,* three contestants were forced to perform in a trio. The three—two women and a man—agreed to meet and practice. One of the females spent time in prayer, asking God to help her win. When practice time came, the second female did not show up but instead spent her time partying with others. When it came time to choose one of the contestants, can you guess who was *not* chosen? That's right—the one who spent time praying.

We all wonder if our faithfulness to God is rewarded. When the stocks of others are rising and ours sink, when our colleagues are promoted and we are let go, or when others seem to succeed and we fail, we can't help but question: does God honor those who are faithful and obedient?

What does it mean to be faithful and obedient to God? Is it when we look, but refrain from touching? Is it when we cheat on our taxes, but not on our spouse? Or is it when we're smart enough not to worship the things in our lives, and worship God instead? When we believe we are being faithful and obedient to God, we question why God allows challenging things to happen in our lives. Moreover, we wonder why we should remain faithful and obedient to a God who doesn't always seem to honor our faithfulness and obedience.

Sometimes, when things go too well for us, we end up forgetting about God. We convince ourselves that we've made it on our own, and that God had no part in our success. There is a scene from the movie *The End,* in which Sonny finds himself out to sea without a boat and trying to swim his way back to shore. When he isn't sure he'll make it, he cries out to God and promises to honor and obey from now on and to go to church and give money. But by the time he is in sight of land and close enough to know he will make it, he has taken all of his promises to God back; in fact, now he is *blaming* God for getting him into that predicament in the first place.

It is not enough to come to church, read our Bibles, or even to pray daily. In the face of our problems, struggles, and the unexpected tragedies in our lives, and when our world seems to be crumbling around us, can we remain faithful and obedient to God? We wonder if God has a plan for our lives. Does God reward faithful obedience to the Divine Word?

Is God concerned about us wherever we are?

Is God concerned about us regardless of our circumstances?

Is God concerned about us, about our lives?

I can tell you this: our obedience and faithfulness do not guarantee us security and rewards in this life. There is no pledge of prosperity, no promise of popularity, no permanent pension plan. We cannot allow ourselves to believe that our success is determined by this world and its standards. But what we can do is hold on to God's unchanging hand and be assured that God is concerned about our world, and about each and every one of us. Even more, God honors those who are faithful and obedient to the Divine Word.

In the words of the old African-American hymn:

> I will trust in the Lord
> I will trust in the Lord
> I will trust in the Lord till I die!

"I will trust in the Lord" is the promise of those who know that God honors those who are faithful and obedient to God. Believe that, and trust!

My faith looks up to Thee,
Thou Lamb of Calvary,
Savior Divine!

Now hear me while I pray,
Take all my sins away,
And let me from this day
Be wholly Thine.

Amen.

25

God Will Take Care of You

No test or temptation that comes your way is beyond the course of what others have had to face. All you need to remember is that God will never let you down; he'll never let you be pushed past your limit; he'll always be there to help you come through it.
(1 Cor. 10:13)

When the little Christian community in Corinth writes to the Apostle Paul, they want him to offer solutions to what they believe are unique challenges as they seek to live Godly lives.

Ships are entering their ports and bringing all kinds of riffraff. Women are behaving immorally, openly and without shame. There are scandals, quarrels, and even drunkenness at the communion table. And they want the Apostle Paul to address their special needs and problems. Contrary to popular opinion, the Bible does not give us neat little blueprints for handling every possible difficulty we meet in life. The Bible does not specialize in perfect formulas telling us how to handle our problems in three easy lessons. So Paul tells the Church at Corinth—and reminds us today—that their problems were not so special at all, but only what they might expect. Others had the same challenges, problems, and issues, including the temptation to throw their hands in the air and give up. In other words, Paul is telling them that there wasn't anything in their situation that Christians ought not to expect in a world like ours, and they might as well get used to those challenges.

Paul's reply must have left an unpleasant taste in their mouths as they read his letter. It isn't too comforting for us to hear, either. We like to think that our situations are unique, the difficulties we have to face a little special. It seems that no one quite understands us and what we have to go through. In fact, for some of us, the only distinction we cling to in life is that our problems are a little more complicated than anyone else's. We may not articulate it, but so often we want to say,

84

You really don't understand what I'm up against.

You don't understand what it's like to work the night shift and get home dog-tired and rarely have an evening home with the family. Do you know what it's like to try and run a business as a Christian and still make a profit in a tough and competitive market? Have you ever faced the prospect of losing your job and not knowing where the money is coming from to pay the rent and the medical bill? Have you ever been bed-ridden for months on end and come to the realization that you are gradually being forgotten by your friends and your family?

But Paul tells the church at Corinth that there are no temptations confronting us that aren't common to all humans. He tells us that God is faithful and does not tempt us above that which we are able to handle. Paul explains that our difficulties are neither unique nor insurmountable, and that God is there to see us through.

God gives us the strength to overcome whatever evil comes our way. Our God is faithful and does not leave us alone. For any test we face, God promises that there is strength available to endure it. God promises to give us strength in the time of trouble, and God's promises are to be trusted. That is why the songwriter Thomas Obediah Chisholm wrote:

> Great is thy Faithfulness,
> O, God my Father.
> There is no shadow of turning with Thee
> You give strength for today
> and bright hope for tomorrow.

God does not remove difficulties from our lives. Instead, God helps us find a way through them.

The cross of Jesus Christ is a pledge and a reminder to each of us that God never promised us an easy way out. We are required to face our challenges and depend on the God of our faith. God wants to remake us into a trusting people. God tells us, "you have to be 'born from above'" (John 3:7). God challenges us to seek first the Kingdom of God, and the rest will be added (Matt. 6:33). This is the God who will see us through, make us better, and lift us up until our problems are resolved.

Whatever our circumstances, the God we serve is able. We must trust in this able God who holds the stars in the sky, keeps land back from the sea, and who cares for us.

Be not dismayed whate'er betide,
God will take care of you;
Beneath His wings of love abide,
God will take care of you.

God will take care of you,
Through every day, over all the way;
He will take care of you,
God will take care of you.[1]

Amen.

1.   Civilla D. Martin, "Be Not Dismayed Whate'er Betide."

About the Author

Reverend Dr. Bernard R. Wilson is the thirty-fifth Senior Minister of the 249-year-old Norfield Congregational Church in Weston, Connecticut. He is the first African American pastor to have been called to this historic church. Dr. Wilson served for twenty-two years as a U.S. Navy chaplain and retired with the rank of Captain. He was Deputy Chaplain of the United States Marine Corps and served as the Navy's Northeast Regional Director of Religious Ministries. He served as the Executive Minister of New York City's Riverside Church and was Interim Senior Minister of the Briarcliff Congregational Church in New York.

Dr. Wilson is widely known as a great preacher and a concerned and compassionate spiritual leader. In 2005, he led a Norfield delegation to Capetown, South Africa, and brought together for the first time tribal and religious leaders, across the color divide, to address issues concerning HIV/AIDS.

Dr. Wilson is married to the former Nereida Torres. They have two sons, Lieutenant Michael B. Wilson, USN, and Daniel B. Wilson, a student at the Massachusetts Institute of Technology. They also have a granddaughter, Mia Jean, upon whom they dote.

978-0-595-39234-6
0-595-39234-2